# MARY M. CERULLO

# SHIPWRECKS

## · EXPLORING SUNKEN CITIES BENEATH THE SEA ·

DUTTON CHILDREN'S BOOKS · *An imprint of Penguin Group (USA) Inc.*

*To Carolee Matsumoto and Clarice Yentsch,*
*two pioneers of science education* —M.C.

## ACKNOWLEDGMENTS

Many thanks for their invaluable help with research to: Clarice M. Yentsch, Corey Malcom, Dylan Kibler, Madeleine Burnside, Melissa Kendrick, Monica Brook, Katie Savale, and Ellen Varella, all of the Mel Fisher Maritime Heritage Museum; Deborah Marx, Matthew Lawrence, and Anne Smrcina of Stellwagen Bank National Marine Sanctuary; Richard Limeburner and Kate Madin of Woods Hole Oceanographic Institution; Dani Fazio and Jamie Rice, Maine Historical Society.

Special appreciation to Carolee Matsumoto, David Gilbertson, Leslie Mansmann, Isabelle Delafosse, and Jeffrey L. Rotman.

Herbert Adams, Deborah Marx, Matthew Lawrence, Richard Limeburner, Corey Malcom, and Clarice Yentsch kindly reviewed all or parts of the manuscript for accuracy. Any mistakes are the author's alone.

Many thanks also to my editor, Rosanne Lauer, and designer Jason Henry.

DUTTON CHILDREN'S BOOKS
A division of Penguin Young Readers Group

Published by the Penguin Group
Penguin Group (USA) Inc., 375 Hudson Street, New York, New York 10014, U.S.A. • Penguin Group (Canada), 90 Eglinton Avenue East, Suite 700, Toronto, Ontario M4P 2Y3, Canada (a division of Pearson Penguin Canada Inc.) • Penguin Books Ltd, 80 Strand, London WC2R 0RL, England • Penguin Ireland, 25 St Stephen's Green, Dublin 2, Ireland (a division of Penguin Books Ltd) • Penguin Group (Australia), 250 Camberwell Road, Camberwell, Victoria 3124, Australia (a division of Pearson Australia Group Pty Ltd) • Penguin Books India Pvt Ltd, 11 Community Centre, Panchsheel Park, New Delhi—110 017, India • Penguin Group (NZ), 67 Apollo Drive, Rosedale, North Shore 0632, New Zealand (a division of Pearson New Zealand Ltd) • Penguin Books (South Africa) (Pty) Ltd, 24 Sturdee Avenue, Rosebank, Johannesburg 2196, South Africa • Penguin Books Ltd, Registered Offices: 80 Strand, London WC2R 0RL, England

Published in the United States by Dutton Children's Books, a division of Penguin Young Readers Group
345 Hudson Street, New York, New York 10014 • www.penguin.com/youngreaders

Designed by Jason Henry
Manufactured in China • First Edition • ISBN: 978-0-525-47968-0 • 10 9 8 7 6 5 4 3 2 1

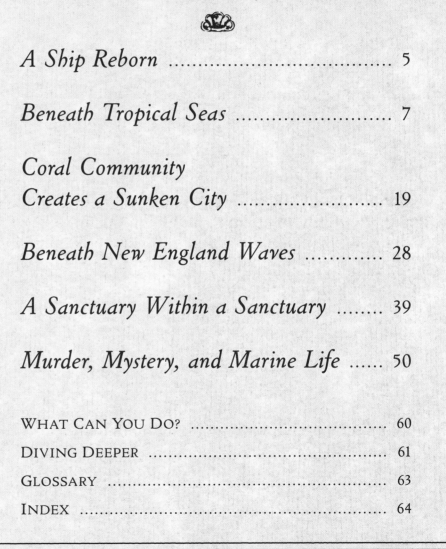

# CONTENTS

# A SHIP REBORN

IMAGINE WHAT IT MUST BE LIKE to be on a sinking ship—raging seas, howling winds, blinding rain, struggling sailors, terrified passengers. The ship shudders one last time as it plunges beneath the waves; moments later, everything is dark and silent. Only pieces of wreckage bobbing on the waves reveal where a ship once had been.

See that same ship lying at the bottom of the sea—broken and half-buried on the ocean floor, cargo and personal belongings strewn across the sand, sharks gliding silently through a splintered hull.

If this image seems tragic, picture that decaying shipwreck years later, a living ocean community, where marine animals have made their home in a sanctuary that suddenly appeared in the vastness of the ocean. We will explore two shipwrecks in two very different places, one in warm water seas and one in frigid New England waters, to see how they were reborn as refuges for the animals and plants in those regions.

A sunken ship is a stroke of good fortune for marine life, if not for the humans aboard it. Shelter is hard to find on the ocean floor, so a shipwreck becomes a magnet for marine creatures. A craft that once carried people above the waves has become a thriving habitat for plants and animals below

LEFT: *Shipwrecks soon become part of the underwater landscape.*

the surface: a shelter for small fish, crabs, and lobsters to hide from their enemies; a pocket of calm water within a restless sea; and a gathering place for marine animals to find food and mates.

History and science come together on the ocean floor. What we find on shipwrecks tells us about the culture and daily life of the passengers and crew. We can learn about another community that followed theirs: the marine life that the shipwreck attracted, a bonus city under the sea. For these reasons, a sunken ship attracts wreck divers, treasure hunters, maritime archaeologists, fishermen, marine biologists—and us.

# BENEATH TROPICAL SEAS

**A** SHIP'S BELL WAS USED TO TELL the time aboard a sailing ship long ago. It was a rung to tell the crew when to change watch, ordering one group to get up for work and the other to rest or eat. A ship's bell was rung to sound the alarm when a pirate flag appeared on the horizon or when mutinous crew members attempted to take over the ship. Surely the ship's bell was rung to call all hands on deck to take down the sails in the face of a worsening storm.

On one unfortunate ship trying to outrun a tropical storm, the ship's bell must have pealed wildly in hurricane-force winds as the ship broke apart on New Ground Reef.

OPPOSITE: *Divers examining the skeleton of a sunken ship.*

LEFT: *The ship's bell finally revealed the name of the mystery ship:* Henrietta Marie.

An hourglass was how the ship's crew kept track of their work schedule, rather like a school bell signals the start and end of the school day.

Hundreds of years ago, every sailing ship had a sandglass that was turned every half hour as the sand ran out. Every time the sandglass was turned, the ship's bell was rung, starting with one stroke at a half hour after midnight. An extra ring of the bell was added each half hour after that. Since shipboard tasks were divided into four-hour watches, the crew changed places every "eight bells." Then the system would begin over again until the next change of watch.

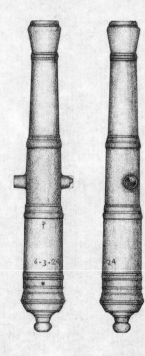

A ship's cannon is revealed.

It was this ship's bell, encrusted with coral, tube worms, and seaweed, which finally revealed the identity of a mystery ship that sank thirty-five miles west of the Florida Keys, a Spanish colony at the southernmost tip of the New World.

The shipwreck was discovered by chance in 1972 by a team of treasure hunters who were searching for the remains of a ship that carried a fortune in silver, gold, and emeralds from the New World to Spain. They found no treasure here, but they did find a priceless piece of history.

The ship lay in pieces on the sandy bottom. Most of the wreck lay in about twenty-five feet of murky water. While sand and fine clay buried much of the hull, coral growth covered the ship's remains. That was fortunate, because any part of the ship's hull that had remained exposed was gone, eaten away by wood-munching teredo worms.

Searchers working with the famous treasure hunter Mel Fisher, based in Key West, Florida, found the hidden ship using a magnetometer towed behind their search ship. The magnetometer, which can detect the presence of iron objects, discovered a cannon covered in coral. According to Corey Malcom, the marine archaeologist who now directs the search, "A magnetometer is a survey tool that measures the variation in the earth's magnetic field. It helped us locate cannons, cannonballs, anchors, and iron bars."

*A blanket of coral hides the identity of this artifact from the* Henrietta Marie.

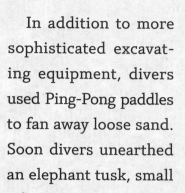

In addition to more sophisticated excavating equipment, divers used Ping-Pong paddles to fan away loose sand. Soon divers unearthed an elephant tusk, small glass beads, thin iron bars, metal drinking cups, and pewter spoons with the portrait of King William III of England on the handles. So this was an English ship, built near the end of the seventeenth century, since King William III had ruled from 1689 to 1702. The wreck had lain on the ocean floor for three centuries. The archaeologists and divers dubbed the nameless ship, "the English wreck."

Then they made a more disturbing discovery: shackles, used to restrain prisoners. Every ship of the time carried them to control unruly crewmen. But as the explorers found more and more shackles, they realized that this was no ordinary ship. They found almost one hundred pairs of leg irons, used to bind prisoners to each other, left foot of one bound to the right foot of his neighbor.

*Utensils used by the crew were discovered under layers of coral growth.*

LEFT: *A curious find*

ABOVE: *Shackles to fit adults and children revealed the purpose of the* Henrietta Marie's *voyage.*

*Ships like the* Henrietta Marie *carried more than twelve million Africans into slavery in the New World.*

Some shackles were so tiny that they could only have fit a child. This clearly had been a slave ship that had carried African captives to the New World.

This ship had been part of the deadly Triangle Trade. Slavers, as they were called, sailed from Europe to the West Coast of Africa to buy African captives, usually captured and sold by rival tribes. The prisoners were stacked belowdecks in row upon row of narrow compartments. The horrific voyage from their homeland to a Caribbean island took about six weeks. More than a quarter of the captives usually died on the trip across the Atlantic Ocean. Many who survived the voyage were sold as slaves and forced to work on a sugar plantation until they died from exhaustion within five to ten years. The sailors and their investors made huge sums of money by selling humans to plantation owners in the New World and by bringing sugar, tobacco, cotton, tropical woods, a blue dye called indigo, and other trade goods back to Europe. The round-trip voyage took about a year.

It is estimated that more than twelve million Africans were kidnapped and delivered to a life of slavery in the New World. That doesn't include the captives who died from disease on the trip across the Atlantic Ocean from their homeland.

Who had died on this ship? Where was the ship going? Had it sold the African captives it must have carried? It took eleven years after the discovery of "the English wreck" to find the key that would lead researchers to the answers to these questions.

The clue was found in an object about fourteen inches tall, discovered by young marine archaeology student David Moore. It was the ship's bell. Most of it was covered in coral growth, but green bronze metal showed through as the diver chipped away at the coating with his fingernail. Slowly, numbers began to appear: 1699. They had just found out when the ship was built! The excited crew used a screwdriver to look for more information. In minutes, the name of the slave ship was revealed: *Henrietta Marie*.

The ship's bell was the key that historians

*Conservator Monica Brook carefully restores the ship's bell to look as it did on the day the Henrietta Marie sank in 1700.*

# MARITIME ARCHAEOLOGISTS
## ✸ STUDY SHIPWRECKS ✸

As a child, Corey Malcom loved finding fossils and rocks. "I had an unconscious call for things from the past," he says. "As archaeologists, when we examine artifacts, we are not so much looking at things, we are looking at people. These things were the building blocks for our modern culture and allow us to feel a connection with those people. Any shipwreck is exciting because of the lessons it can teach us. You can view one object from so many different angles: for what it represents for technology of the day, its artistic value, what it tells you about cultural changes, values, and religion of the time.

"To be an archaeologist, you cannot have a short attention span. Studying a shipwreck consumes a big chunk of your life. Amongst all the details, it has to be looked at from artistic, technological, and cultural angles. A hundred years from now someone could be looking at the *Henrietta Marie* from a new angle that nobody has even thought of yet."

*Marine archaeologist Corey
Malcom makes a find.*

needed to unlock her story. With the name of the English wreck now known, *Henrietta Marie*'s history could be traced, along with that of many of those who sailed on her. Researchers went to London to look through historical shipping records, maps, written histories, business contracts, wills, and other documents. They found the ship's manifests, which listed the people and goods taken on board. The names of crew members and their wills were discovered.

Captain Thomas Chamberlain led a crew of perhaps twelve to eighteen men on the voyage that went astray on a reef off the coast of Florida. Financial records showed that they had off-loaded one hundred ninety captives in Jamaica to work on the sugar plantations: ninety men, sixty women, thirty boys, and ten girls, all from the Ibo Tribe in what is now eastern Nigeria. They had sold the Africans for over 3,000 pounds in English money. Today, that would be worth about $400,000.

No matter what profit Captain Chamberlain and his crew made from selling their human cargo, they never got to spend their fortune. The records in London showed that the ship sank in 1700. Marine archaeologist Corey Malcom said, "We'll never know why the ship sank. We know it left Jamaica in

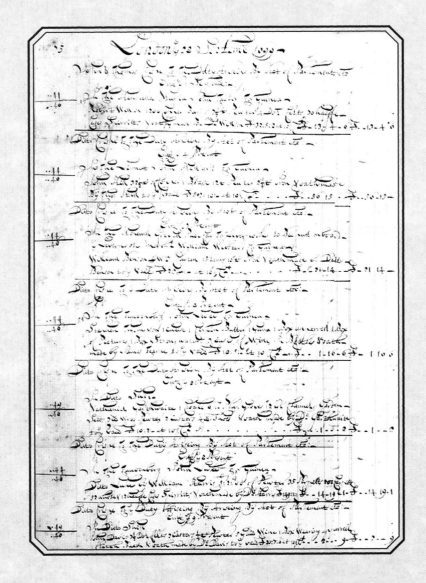

*Records of the* Henrietta Marie *were found in London.*

June. From the violence of the wreck and the time of year, we suspect it was a hurricane. It was so badly broken up and scattered that we think it must have hit the reef in a storm."

Had the *Henrietta Marie* survived its encounter with New Ground Reef, it might have had a second life as a pirate ship. Because slave ships were sturdy and fast in order to get as many of their human cargo as possible delivered alive, they were a favorite target of pirates looking to upgrade their transports. The slave ship's crew, once captured, could convert to piracy, be set adrift in a small boat, or murdered.

The *Henrietta Marie* is the only slave ship

to have been found and documented in the Western Hemisphere. As more of the wreck was explored, more artifacts were discovered that attested to the ship's dark past. In all, more than 7,500 objects were found around the wreck site. The divers picked up many thin iron bars. They were only about twelve inches long and two inches wide. At first they could not figure out what these pieces of cheap metal could have been used for. Other ships' records of slave trading with African tribal leaders revealed the purpose of these iron bars. Thirteen bars bought a man, nine a woman, and proportionately less acquired a boy or a girl, depending on their age. Corey Malcom felt the weight of history when he picked up the thin iron bars. "It's haunting to think you would buy people with those little bars." The dive team found glass beads, pewter dishes, guns, and swords that were also used to trade for humans in Africa.

None of the African captives were aboard the *Henrietta Marie* when it sank, but reminders of their existence kept appearing in the shipwreck. Divers excavated a huge

OPPOSITE: *The ribs of the sunken ship seem ghostly in the murky water.*

LEFT: *Iron bars were used to buy captives in Africa.*

copper kettle from which the captives would have eaten a meager meal of watery porridge twice a day. For Corey, it was one of the artifacts from the slave ship that affected him the most. "This copper cauldron sustained all those people throughout the voyage."

When the marine archaeologists found it, it was encrusted with coral and sand. After three hundred years on the ocean floor, the huge cauldron had become part of the underwater scenery.

# CORAL COMMUNITY CREATES A SUNKEN CITY

CORALS AND OTHER ENCRUSTING plants and animals have totally transformed what little remains of the *Henrietta Marie*, converting it into an underwater condominium for thousands of marine animals and plants. Hard corals and soft corals now cover the spot where the shipwreck lays. Teredo worms have eaten all the wood that was above the seafloor, so what does remain of the hull—perhaps only five percent—is buried beneath the sand. Pieces of the wreck and its cargo were scattered by waves and currents. Those have been disguised by coral growth, wedged between crevices in the reef or buried under the sand.

What we usually think of as a coral reef is a complex of tiny coral animals living in limestone houses cemented to other stony structures built by generations of corals that lived before them. Coral reefs are literally cities under the sea. Some are larger than any human-built metropolis on earth. They are the work of massive construction crews of pea-size animals, each of which looks like a cup surrounded with tentacles. The coral animal, called a polyp, extracts a chemical dissolved in the seawater—calcium carbonate—and transforms it into a hard limestone shell. Living within the polyp are microscopic plants called zooxanthellae. These tiny plants convert the energy of sunlight into food for themselves and for their coral hosts, and a side effect of this process helps the polyp build its shell. Because these corals build hard, stony skeletons, they are called "hard corals." The polyps withdraw into their stone sanctuaries during the day. They poke their stinging tentacles out of their fortresses at night to snatch food floating in the seawater.

RIGHT: *A coral reef—or a shipwreck—provides a place for sponges, oysters, anemones, and seaweeds to anchor.*

OPPOSITE: *A barrel sponge can grow large enough to hide a human!*

A few brain corals and boulder corals—hard corals—dot the ocean floor around the wreck site and cover pieces of the debris from the ship, but branching corals, such as staghorn corals, apparently aren't able to withstand the strong currents that stream through the area. Better adapted to the turbulent water are soft corals with names like sea whips and sea fans. These soft corals have flexible skeletons that bend and sway in the ocean currents.

Other animals that need a hard surface to hold onto also festoon the *Henrietta Marie*. Oysters, sponges, sea anemones, and feathery sea star relatives called crinoids have set up residence on the remains of the ship. Some of the sponges, called barrel sponges, are big enough for a diver to stand inside, but the scientists know that these very old sponges shouldn't be trampled on. These animals work hard pumping hundreds of gallons of seawater through their systems each day to filter out food and oxygen to live. Decorator crabs pluck off bits of seaweed and sponges and glue them onto their backs, in order to camouflage themselves against the wreckage. In contrast, candy-cane shrimp advertise themselves with their bright red-and-white stripes, earning them the nickname of barber-pole shrimp. They set up cleaning stations where fish, even including moray eels, come to have parasites picked off their bodies. The candy-cane shrimp are happy to oblige. The parasites that annoy the fish are delicacies to the shrimp.

The *Henrietta Marie* lies within an area of the Gulf of Mexico that often has steady

As a parrot fish scrapes off the hard coral with its teeth shaped like a parrot's beak, it makes a gnawing sound that carries a long distance underwater.

you are concentrating on finding objects buried in the sand."

Although divers are careful to work in pairs, one may feel very alone when one's partner is not in sight. Ordinary noises seem louder and stranger, like the creaking sounds a house makes as it settles in the middle of the night. The sound of a parrot fish gnawing on the reef carries for quite a distance underwater. Its teeth have fused together to make a strong beak that can break open the hard coral skeletons to get to the microscopic plants inside the coral polyps. Snapping shrimp, too, can make quite a racket as they snap one giant, outsized claw. It's loud enough to scare away a would-be predator.

The murkiness of the water around the bones of the *Henrietta Marie* can present real dangers for the divers, making every encounter a surprise. On one occasion, a large bull shark buzzed a diver. Bull sharks are heavyset, cartilaginous fish that eat almost anything, including other sharks and stingrays. They are as likely to attack humans as are great white sharks and tiger sharks.

ocean currents. Corey, who has spent more than fifteen years exploring the wreck, says, "The reef here is very beautiful, but the water is not terribly clear. It's not an easy place to dive. On some days there is one-hundred-feet visibility, but about half the time, waves and currents make the water quite murky. Sometimes you can only get your bearings by listening to the reef crack and the parrot fish nibbling on the coral. It can be quite eerie to have almost zero visibility when

Another time, one of the explorers was so intent on mapping the debris field that he ignored someone nudging him from behind as he crouched on the seafloor. When he turned around, he discovered it wasn't one of his dive team urging him to move, but a nurse shark intent on getting to the spot that he was examining. A nurse shark prefers to spend most of its time lying motionless on the ocean floor; this one evidently wanted to be right where the diver was working. A nurse shark can sense potential prey in the sand with two whisker-like appendages called barbels. It will also put its mouth against a crevice in a reef or shipwreck to literally vacuum a victim from its hiding place. Small, grinding teeth easily crush the shells of crabs, shrimp, and spiny lobsters.

*A nurse shark lies on the ocean floor.*

Oftentimes silvery barracuda glide by to investigate anything unusual in their area of the ocean. Their razor-sharp teeth and low-slung jaws give them a sinister look, but barracuda rarely attack humans. Most attacks, however, take place in murky water, just like the turbulent seas that surround the *Henrietta Marie*.

A giant grouper also shows up on occasion.

Although more curious than aggressive, a giant grouper, by its size alone, can make a diver nervous. It may weigh more than twice as much as a human, and it can open its cavernous mouth amazingly wide in order to swallow very large prey. Giant groupers, also called Goliath groupers, have been known to follow divers for hours, nibbling at their flippers.

*A giant grouper is a curious fish that often comes to watch what the divers are doing.*

The biggest danger to divers excavating the shipwreck is from a much smaller source: fire coral. Although it lives among the brain corals and sea fans on the reef, it is not a true coral. It is a colony of small animals called hydroids, which are relatives of jellyfish and sea anemones. Like its larger cousins, fire coral has stinging cells that can leave painful welts on uncovered skin. Fortunately, fire coral is easy to spot because of its bright color.

If you were to go diving near the shipwreck on a day when the water was clear, then you would see the true jewels of the *Henrietta Marie*. Ruby, emerald, and sapphire are the vibrant colors that gleam from the many small fishes that visit the wreck. Many-colored queen angelfish, butterfly fish, damselfish, and yellowtail snappers are just some of the five hundred species of fish that inhabit the reefs around the Florida Keys.

Among tropical fishes, bright colors are an effective way to advertise for a mate or warn away a competitor that tries to invade one's space. Even with their neon colors,

many of these coral reef fishes have ways to disguise themselves from their enemies. The four-eyed butterfly fish, for instance, sports what looks like an enormous black eye on its tail, but it is a fake. A black stripe runs across its real eye, helping to divert attention to the eyespot on its tail. A predator is likely to attack the fake eye, which allows the butterfly fish to escape by darting away in the opposite direction.

*One of the biggest dangers around the wreck site is fire coral, which can inflict a painful sting.*

Sometimes divers visit the *Henrietta Marie* at night, when they get to see an entirely different community of animals swarming around the shipwreck. Snappers, squirrelfish, and grunts hide by day and emerge at night to feed. They swim past a sleeping parrot fish, nestled inside a mucous bubble it has secreted from beneath its scales. This "sleeping bag" seals its scent from predators. Spiny lobsters march across the seafloor in single file to forage among the seagrass beds. Crinoids, relatives of sea stars, unfurl their delicate arms at night to trap plankton on their sticky tube feet.

As the divers sweep their hands through the water, they create trails of light by triggering tiny plants—phytoplankton—to create their own living light. Why do these bioluminescent plants blink like fireflies in the night ocean? One guess is that that they may be trying to startle predators, but no one really knows why they use their energy to make such a scene. Whatever the reason, they add to the mystery of the *Henrietta Marie* and its occupants from the past and present.

# BENEATH NEW ENGLAND WAVES

THE *HENRIETTA MARIE* SANK AT the southern tip of what is now the United States. It was heading back home to England, a voyage of several weeks and thousands of miles. Another ship was traveling along the coast of New England. Its journey of a hundred miles to its home port should have taken only ten hours. One sailed through warm, tropical seas, the other through cold ocean water, where any sailor who fell overboard could survive for only a few minutes in its chilly grip. The *Henrietta Marie* probably met its fate in a hurricane; the other ship sank in a fierce winter snowstorm.

The two ships were also a world apart for their passengers. Most of those who sailed on the *Henrietta Marie* were prisoners, and even the crew had to put up with miserable living conditions. It was barely ninety feet long and packed up to three hundred captives at a time below its decks. The other ship, over three times the length of the *Henrietta Marie*, had many decks and could accommodate up to eight hundred passengers in style. Those who made the journey on this ship were treated to every luxury of the day. Even the crew members, many of whom were descended from black slaves, wore their uniforms with pride and earned good wages.

Maine

Portland

Massachusetts

*THE PORTLAND*

. Atlantic Ocean .

N

W          E

S

. Gulf of Mexico .

Florida

*HENRIETTA MARIE*

Florida Keys

*Two shipwrecks separated by nearly 2,000 miles and two centuries.*

29

Unlike the *Henrietta Marie*, the name of the northern ship was well known. The ferocious winter storm that sank it also destroyed four hundred other ships and boats, and killed more than 450 people on land and at sea, but the storm was forever remembered as "The Portland Gale," because it sank the famous steamship, the *Portland*.

Stars glimmered in the early evening sky on Saturday, November 26, 1898, as passengers boarded the luxurious paddle-wheel steamer *Portland* in Boston, Massachusetts, bound for Portland, Maine, the city after which the ship was named. An overnight voyage was scheduled to bring the nearly two hundred eager passengers and crew back to Maine by dawn the next day. Many were returning from spending Thanksgiving in Boston; several families carried the presents they'd purchased for the upcoming Christmas holiday.

The *Portland* was built with luxury and

*Photograph of the
S.S.* Portland

profit in mind. It had a domed skylight in its main salon, carved mahogany furniture, and velvet carpets. Passage cost one dollar, but those who wanted sleeping quarters for the overnight voyage paid another dollar for a white pine cabin or three dollars more for a cherry-paneled stateroom. None of those luxuries helped the ship withstand the night's hurricane-force winds and towering waves.

Despite forecasts of an approaching storm, the *Portland* left its berth at India Wharf at precisely 7:00 P.M. on the evening of November 26, 1898. Being on time and making good time were important virtues on the cusp of the twentieth century; punctuality was the proof of efficiency and progress in an increasingly mobile society. Thanks to the development of steam-powered ships and railroad trains, more people than ever before delighted in the adventure of travel.

This elegant "overnight boat," as it was called, carried its passengers to their destination while they slept. All who boarded it were impressed by its lavish decor, highly

prized in this Victorian age. It was different from other oceangoing ships of its day. Most were being built of iron, but the hull of the *Portland* was made of wood by Maine craftsmen, known as the best wooden boat builders in the world. It floated in the water rather like an iceberg in reverse. Most of an iceberg is submerged below the water's surface, but the *Portland* rode high out of the water. Its draft, or the part of the hull below the waterline, was very shallow; only ten feet of the hull was underwater, making it fairly unstable for the stormy seas off the

*A magazine of the day depicted the glamour of the* Portland *with a drawing of the grand salon with its "dome being lighted with colored glass."*

coast of New England. The ship was propelled by two thirty-five-foot-tall paddle wheels mounted on opposite sides of the ship. This arrangement made it less maneuverable than sleeker vessels with propellers in the back. Yet, for eight years, the ship had safely navigated the one hundred miles of open ocean between Boston and Portland.

The ship had barely passed the protecting islands of Boston Harbor when the seas began to roll and a monster snowstorm bore down on the vessel. It was a classic nor'easter, named for the winds that blow in from the Northeast and drive the storm up the East Coast. Nor'easters are notorious for producing strong winds, heavy rain or snow, and gigantic waves. Meteorologists estimated that the wind blew at forty-five miles an hour throughout the night, at times gusting to over ninety miles an hour, well above hurricane strength. Waves ran over thirty feet high. Time stopped for the floating city.

The steamship *Portland* did not arrive in Portland, Maine, the next morning. By that evening, though, the first remains of the ship began to wash ashore on Cape Cod, Massachusetts, a sandy stretch of land thrust out into Massachusetts Bay like a bent arm. Residents of the Cape found life jackets and ice-cream cans, soon followed by fragments of the ship and the bodies of some of the passengers and crew. Only forty bodies were recovered. A passenger's pocket watch showed nine-thirty, as the time when time stopped for all the estimated one hundred ninety-two passengers and crew aboard. In all, four watches washed ashore; all had stopped within minutes of each other. They documented when the huge nor'easter drove the luxurious passenger ship to the bottom of the Atlantic.

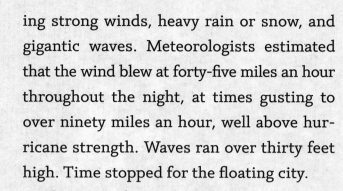

*Several watches washed ashore from the* Portland. *All of them had stopped within minutes of each other—around 9:30.*

The storm washed away coastal buildings, railroad lines, and telegraph wires, so that news of the fate of the ship and its passengers didn't reach Portland for several days. For weeks after, friends and relatives waited for news about their loved ones, since they couldn't even be sure who was aboard the *Portland* when it sank. The only complete list of passengers and crew went down with the ship.

At the close of the nineteenth century, the sinking of a large passenger ship like the *Portland* made headlines just as the crash of a jumbo jet would today. Newspapers reported that debris from the vessel was strewn over many miles of the Massachusetts coast, making it hard to pinpoint the location where the ship foundered. Two weeks after the *Portland* disappeared, the *Boston Globe* newspaper sponsored a search for the remains of the ship, but its resting place stayed a mystery for over ninety years. They stretched chains between two boats to drag along the ocean floor, but repeated searches did not reveal the resting place of the *Portland*.

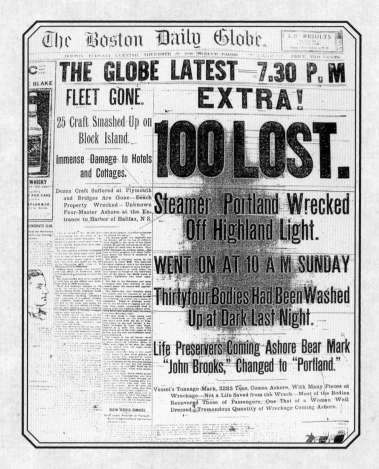

In 1978, two avid shipwreck hunters, Arnold Carr and John Fish of the Historical Maritime Group of New England, set out to find the *Portland*. They researched information on ocean currents and read historical newspaper accounts of the disaster to help them figure out where the ship might be found. They pored through newspaper

*The sinking of the* Portland *made headlines around the country.*

## ❈ SIDE-SCAN SONAR ❈

Sonar, short for SOund NAvigation Ranging, sends beams of sound toward the seafloor that bounce back like echoes. Since the speed of sound is known, the depth can be calculated by figuring out how long it takes for sounds to reflect back from objects, like rocks and shipwrecks, on the ocean floor. The sonar converts the reflected sound's strength to different shades of gray to create black-and-white images of what is on the seafloor.

accounts and eyewitness interviews of Cape Cod residents to make a record of when and where debris from the wreckage had washed up along the shores of Cape Cod. For years, they spent many weekends on their boat, crisscrossing the ocean waters near where the first wreckage from the *Portland* was found, searching the ocean floor with a magnetometer and a side-scan sonar.

Finally, after nearly ten years of unsuccessful searching, the explorers turned to Richard Limeburner, a scientist at Woods Hole Oceanographic Institution on Cape Cod. Richard Limeburner is an oceanographer who studies ocean currents. John Fish and Arnie Carr provided him with all they had learned about when and where wreckage from the ship was found. Limeburner made a computer model of how ocean currents and storm winds might have moved the debris from the *Portland*'s wreck site. The most intriguing clue was the time that the watches had stopped. Richard Limeburner identified two search sites: one if the vessel sank at 9:30 P.M. and another if it had gone down at 9:30 A.M.

# ❄ OCEANOGRAPHERS FIGURE OUT HOW THE OCEAN WORKS ❄

Richard Limeburner is a physical oceanographer. He studies ocean currents, mostly around coastal areas. He explains his work: "The energy of the sun, the atmosphere, and the tides create ocean currents. We observe and measure ocean currents and make a computer model that can help predict what will happen in a larger region."

Understanding ocean currents helps marine biologists predict if young fish such as cod and haddock, which float in the ocean currents, will find enough food—other floating plankton—for the baby fish to survive. When there is an oil spill, cleanup crews need to know where the currents will spread the oil in order to contain the spill. That information tells them where to set up booms, or floating barriers, to protect beaches and salt marshes.

Knowing where the currents are coming from and going helps search-and-rescue operations find ships and people lost at sea. A few years before he helped to find the *Portland*, Richard Limeburner was asked to aid in the search for a helicopter that had crashed into the ocean during a flight from New York City to the island of Nantucket, just south of Cape Cod. The three young men aboard were missing, and their families begged searchers to find their bodies. Three pieces of the drifting wreckage provided the only evidence of where the helicopter might have crashed. The oceanographer used the locations of where the debris had been found and his knowledge of wind, tides, and currents to map where the pieces may have come from. He suggested a place on the ocean floor where their projected paths would have crossed. Within thirty minutes of arriving at that location, a search team found the downed helicopter.

ABOVE: *Oceanographer Richard Limeburner studied the ocean currents to pinpoint the location of the* Portland *after others had searched unsuccessfully for nearly a hundred years.*

Using the oceanographer's computer model, Arnold Carr and John Fish finally located the wreck. It lay in over three hundred feet of water. The spot where the ship sank was many miles farther north than anyone else had searched. It corresponded with the location that the computer model had predicted if the ship had sunk at 9:30 at night, Richard explained, "The nor'easter's one-hundred-mile-an-hour winds and waves breaking over the shallow banks of Stellwagen Bank would have created a strong current that would have pushed the debris along very quickly."

OPPOSITE: *Marine archaeologist Deborah Marx checks out two important research tools: the side-scan sonar towfish (yellow) and magnetometer (orange). They will help searchers explore the* Portland, *lying on the ocean floor more than 300 feet below them.*

The last moments of the *Portland* were now known.

Learning what the last few hours must have been like for the passengers and crew had to wait a few more years. Although it was technically possible for a diver to reach that depth, strong ocean currents, the icy darkness of deep water, and unpredictable weather make it dangerous to attempt to dive to the site. In 2002, the Stellwagen Bank National Marine Sanctuary and the National Undersea Research Center for the North Atlantic and Great Lakes at the University of Connecticut joined in the search. From the deck of a state-of-the-art research vessel, scientists deployed side-scan sonar and a robot vehicle to confirm that the ship Carr and Fish had located was indeed the *Portland*.

Piloted by remote control by an operator using a joystick aboard the Research Vessel *Connecticut*, an underwater robot, ROV *Hela*, explored the hull of the ship. The operator aboard the *Connecticut* was careful not to let this "robot on a leash" become entangled in the abandoned fishing nets that draped the hull of the *Portland*. Fishermen chasing schools of fish often snagged their nets on the pieces of the shipwreck that protruded above the ocean floor.

Equipped with lights and video cameras, the ROV—short for Remotely Operated Vehicle—transmitted back images of the wreckage that matched antique photographs and paintings of the *Portland*. The ship sits upright on the ocean floor, with almost its entire two-hundred-ninety-foot hull visible. Parts of the ship, such as a steam release pipe and a ceramic toilet, lie nearby.

The most curious feature is something that resembles a giant seesaw protruding through the exposed deck fifty feet above the seafloor. The structure was once the machinery that transferred the up-and-down motion of the steam engine's piston into a circular motion to rotate the paddle wheels. It was called the "walking beam." The skeleton of the walking beam resembles a character from a Transformer movie.

When the ship was intact, the walking beam would have sat above the *Portland*'s highest deck, known as the hurricane deck.

*The National Undersea Research Center at the University of Connecticut launched the ROV* Hela *to explore the wreck of the steamship* Portland.

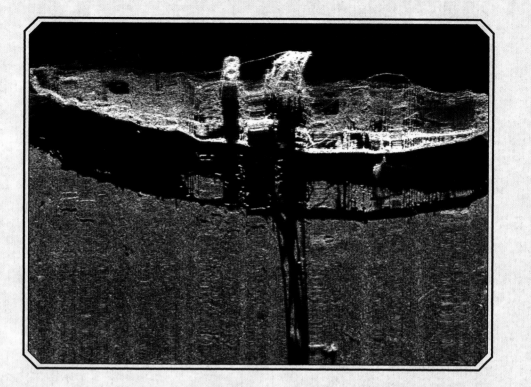

Side-scan sonar image of the Portland *showing the boiler uptakes and walking beam projecting above the wreck.*

The steamship was built with four decks (hurricane, saloon, main, and lower cabin), but now the two upper decks are missing. Rows of luxury cabins and the pilothouse, where the captain commanded the ship, have disappeared. Yet remarkably, fragile panes of glass lay unbroken nearby. Stacks of teacups and saucers rest undamaged, although caked in mud, in what once was the kitchen. A large ceramic mug is perched on the wreckage next to twisted steam pipes as if someone had just set it down to run an errand.

To those who know how to read the clues, the state of the hull and the debris tell a chilling story about the ship's last few hours. Deborah Marx and Matthew Lawrence, maritime archaeologists with Stellwagen Bank National Marine Sanctuary, believe that the decks did not wash away all at once. More likely, smaller pieces of the ship were ripped off by ferocious winds and waves throughout the evening. Imagine the horror of the people on board as they watched—or heard—parts of the ship's bridge and cabins being swept away.

The sea was too rough to launch the lifeboats. At some point, the electric lights, a modern convenience that had recently replaced most of the oil lamps, may have gone out, leaving the passengers and crew in darkness. As the upper decks were torn away, the hull was exposed to the waves. After many long hours, the ship's exposed hull probably filled with water, swamped by waves like a bathtub toy. It gently drifted down to settle intact on the ocean floor.

# A SANCTUARY WITHIN A SANCTUARY

**T**HE *PORTLAND*, WHICH SANK OFF the coast of Massachusetts in 1898, is now home to cod, cusk, pollock, and flounder.

The *Portland* lies within the boundaries of Stellwagen Bank National Marine Sanctuary, which covers 842 square miles of ocean between Cape Ann and Cape Cod, Massachusetts. A marine sanctuary is rather like an offshore national park. Visitors are welcome, but they must abide by rules that protect the wildlife and cultural resources.

In fact, visitors have been coming to Stellwagen Bank since before the United States was founded, to pursue the whales and fish that thrived there. Stellwagen Bank National Marine Sanctuary was created in 1992, primarily to protect the whales, many of them in danger of extinction, that visit the coast of New England each summer to indulge in the abundant seafood.

*Even fragile teacups and dishware in the galley survived the* Portland's *plummet to the seafloor.*

The cold waters off the New England coast are a giant food factory. Sunlight shining into the shallow waters of Stellwagen Bank creates an ideal underwater greenhouse. Minerals washed in by rivers from the land, as well as decaying plants and animals that sank to the ocean floor, provide the fertilizer for tiny plants called *phytoplankton*—microscopic floating plants—to bloom. These plants are eaten by unimaginably large numbers of tiny animals, *zooplankton*, which in turn, feed the fishes and whales or the animals they eat.

The *Portland* has become a refuge and a residence for the marine life that inhabits these cold waters. It has become a haven for fish that would normally pass through the area. The ship provides a stable surface for animals such as sponges and sea anemones to attach to permanently.

Each year since 2002, sanctuary scientists have returned to the site of the *Portland*, exploring new areas and documenting changes to the shipwreck. Marine archaeologists would love to explore the interior of the ship with the ROV, but fishing nets drape almost the entire hull, preventing the robot from getting too close. Too heavy to move or cut away, the nets could easily ensnare the sub as they once captured fish. Someday, a smaller, more maneuverable ROV may be built that can safely enter the hidden depths of the *Portland*, where it will undoubtedly find even more artifacts, and possibly even human remains.

The lights of the ROV reveal a scene that resembles a fierce snowstorm battering the deck of the *Portland*, a reminder of the one that sank the ship in 1898. This time, though, it is a blizzard of plankton, tiny life-forms, as thick as soup even at this depth. The fish can hear the approaching vehicle's propellers

BELOW: *Marine anemones and other sea life have settled on the hull next to the "bitts," structures that were used to tie the ship to the piers in Boston and Portland.*

OPPOSITE: *Map of the Stellwagen Bank National Marine Sanctuary.*

and see its bright lights. Some hide inside the *Portland*, but more come out to greet the robot as the arrival of the ROV launches a feeding frenzy. Zooplankton—tiny animals such as newly hatched fish and crabs, as well as shrimp and arrowworms—swarm around the beams from the lamps of the robot like moths around a porch light. Arrowworms, although only about three-quarters of an inch long, have powerful jaws that can devour baby fish as long as themselves. These tiny animals, in turn, draw hungry fishes of all sizes, which ignore the lights and cameras of the floating robot to gobble down an unexpected meal.

Fishes are the crew of the *Portland* now. The undisputed captain of the shipwreck is the cod. It sits quietly on the deck rippling its fins, as if keeping tabs on all that goes on under its watch. Besides being the largest fish on the wreck, it sports a distinctive chin whisker, called a barbel, which it uses to detect prey on the ocean floor. The barbel can feel and taste what's on the sand, although not always accurately, as Styrofoam cups have been found inside cods' stomachs!

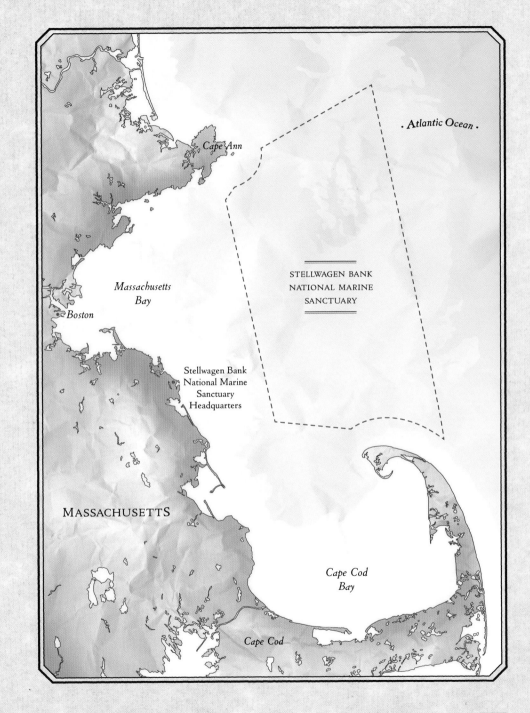

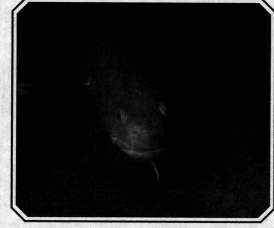

*Shown above, left to right, are cod, pollock and cusk.*

The fish here aren't the crayon-colored varieties that you'd see swimming around the *Henrietta Marie*. These New Englanders are typically less flashy, more muted, than their Caribbean cousins. Here, speckled bodies mimic the colors of the sand and gravel on the ocean floor, or silvery scales reflect back the light, like waves on water. What these fish may lack in loud colors, they make up for in impressive size. Fish up to three feet long are common on the wreck.

Many of the fish resemble each other, because they are members of the same family. The cod is the largest member of a family that includes pollock, haddock, hake, and cusk. Cod can grow to be over four feet long

and weigh one hundred pounds, the size of an elementary school student. No wonder they are said to swim in schools! (Actually, the term "school" comes from a Dutch word meaning a "crowd.")

Pollock, a slate-gray version of the cod, dart about the deck while cod glide calmly through holes in the hull or sit on the main deck watching the ROV approach. Pollock have run right into the ROV as they race after arrowworms.

Cusk have taken up their post at the bow of the ship and have been seen in the same place year after year when the expedition returns. The fins of the cusk form a continuous ribbon around the fish, giving it an eel-like look. Like many of the fishes here, cusk can change color. When cusk get excited, dark brown stripes appear on their backs. Another curious feature of these fishes is that many of them, including the cusk, cod, and pollock, can make sounds. Recordings of fish noises sound like grunts, squeaks, and croaks.

A flounder, another resident of the wreck site, doesn't look like any of the other fish. A flounder is the very definition of a flatfish. This bottom-dweller nestles into the sand on the seafloor until only its eyes, which both happen to be on the same side of its head, peek out above the sand. It can change its skin color to perfectly camouflage itself against the sand or gravel of the seafloor. When it's born, a flounder looks like a normal fish, but after about six weeks, one eye begins to move across the skull until it joins

*Flounder.*

the other. Then it even begins to swim sideways, so that one side is up and the other faces the ocean floor. Depending on which side becomes the "up" side, the fish can be a "right-handed" or a "left-handed" flounder.

Cod, pollock, cusk, and flounder are called groundfish because they usually can be found living near the ocean floor. Fishing boats drag cone-shaped trawl nets that are pulled across the ocean floor with weights and rollers to catch these bottom huggers. A cod can outrun a fishing net for perhaps ten minutes before it tires and is scooped up into the net. It becomes trapped in a bag at the back of the net, appropriately called the *cod end.*

Although fishermen prefer to chase schools of fish across a flat seafloor, they know that fish congregate around "hangs," like boulders and shipwrecks. Sometimes fishermen get too close to these obstructions and entangle their gear, as they have on the *Portland*. These "ghost" fishing nets float just above the ocean floor, continuing to trap fish. Crabs scurry across the nets feeding on the dead and decaying fish entangled in the mesh.

Acadian redfish "hide" from the ROV by staying very still. The ROV can get within five feet of their perch inside the crevices of the walking beam before they will move. They do not need the light from the robot

*Redfish also have found a home in the* Portland.

# ❋ Cod Helped Shape American History ❋

Cod once ruled the whole of Stellwagen Bank, in fact, all of the northeastern coast of North America. They were once so plentiful that fishermen claimed that they could walk across their backs. Quite possibly the first visitor to explore the wrecked *Portland* after it sank was a codfish.

In 1602, an English sailor exploring the New World was so "pestered by cod" that he named the arm of land that extended into the ocean "Cape Cod." John Smith, who became famous for helping to settle the colony of Virginia, charted the coastline of New England and used the name on his map. In 1614, he caught forty-seven thousand cod and sold them to Spain.

The Pilgrims arrived in North America in 1620 and established a settlement they called Plymouth near Cape Cod. They came looking for religious freedom. What they found was a fortune in fish. In 1650, the colonists sold 300,000 salted cod to Europe, especially to Catholic countries such as Spain and Portugal where much of the population ate fish on Fridays. Cod made many of the new arrivals rich and established New England as an important commercial center. A wooden codfish, known as "the sacred cod," hangs in the state capitol building in Boston, Massachusetts, a symbol of the fortunes that were made by the fishermen and merchants who traded in cod.

Cod also played an important role in the Triangle Trade. While high-quality fish was sold to European diners, the lowest quality cod was sold to Caribbean plantation owners to feed their slaves.

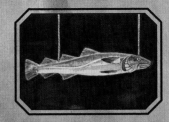

*A statue of a cod hangs in the State House in Boston, a tribute to its importance in the founding of Massachusetts.*

---

to see their surroundings. Their huge eyes reveal that they are deepwater dwellers. Their large eyes can take in what little light penetrates the deep water. Redfish are believed to be able to live for a hundred years. Having lived so long, it is not surprising, perhaps, that they are not bothered by the sight of an alien visitor with "eyes" even bigger than their own.

Every inch of the shipwreck teems with life. From a distance, the colorful sea anemones make it appear as if the hull is covered with white and orange polka dots. Shrimp, sea stars, spider crabs, and rock crabs tiptoe across the decks and down the sides of the ship, while frilled sea anemones, branching hydroids, and sponges provide shelter for young fish, such as Atlantic cod

and Acadian redfish. Snake blennies, slender fish with fins that run the length of their bodies, wriggle among sponges with names like deadman's fingers, sulfur sponge, and bread-crumb sponge.

What would a shipwreck be without a shark patrolling it? The most common shark in the Stellwagen Bank National Marine Sanctuary is the dogfish shark. Although it grows to be only about two to three feet long, it has a reputation as a vicious and destructive fish. Acting like a pack of wild dogs, a school of dogfish will attack more fish than the sharks can eat. Spiny dogfish are voracious predators of adult cod.

Another local shark, the basking shark, grows to be much bigger, up to forty feet long, but it is totally different in its behavior. The basking shark gets its name because it normally spends much of its time sunning itself at the water's surface. Its tiny teeth are useless for attacking any creatures larger than zooplankton or small fish, which it catches on small hooks on its gills, called *gill rakers*.

One visitor that may alarm both humans

and beasts is a great white shark. The great white is not common anywhere, but it roams the cool waters of the world's oceans. It sometimes will pursue its prey right up to the shoreline. Although great white sharks may come together to feed on the same prey, such as seals or sea lions, they usually travel alone.

Leatherback sea turtles, regular summer visitors to Stellwagen Bank, can easily explore the shipwreck. They often dive deeper than 1,000 feet and have been known to reach a depth of 3,900 feet.

Stellwagen Bank has been named one of the ten best whale-watching sites in the world by *USA Today*. One of the premier

OPPOSITE: *A basking shark feeds in the plankton-rich waters of Stellwagen Bank.*

ABOVE: *Leatherback sea turtles like this one visit Stellwagen Bank. Scientists track its migration path with the satellite tag attached like a backpack. Every time the turtle surfaces to breathe, the antenna transmits its location to a satellite 22,000 miles overhead.*

attractions for whale watchers is the humpback whale. The most acrobatic of whales, the humpback frequently launches itself out of the water headfirst or smacks its tail forcefully on the water's surface. Both actions result in a huge splash and a thunderous crash. When it slaps its long white side flippers on the water, one can appreciate how it got its elegant scientific name of *Megaptera novaeangliae*, or "big-winged New Englander." Humpbacks feed on sand lance and herring, which feed on zooplankton, which are plentiful here. Whale watchers might also catch a glimpse of fin whales, sei whales, minke whales, and Atlantic white-sided dolphins.

More rarely seen, because they are the most endangered whales in the world, are the northern right whales. Whale hunters in centuries past called them the "right whales" to hunt because they were slow, full of blubber for making lamp oil, and their carcasses didn't sink after they were killed. Biologists estimate that eighty thousand of these whales once roamed the oceans. Today, partly as a result of the success of those whalers, there are only about three hundred northern right whales left in the world. Northern right whales are listed as an "endangered species," meaning its population is so small that it is in immediate risk of becoming extinct. Each year, some are killed by being struck by large ships or by becoming entangled in fishing nets. Scientists and conservationists know each surviving right whale by name and celebrate every time a right whale calf is born.

# MURDER, MYSTERY, AND MARINE LIFE

WHILE WHALING WAS NO LONGER one of the major industries of New England at the time that the *Portland* sank, many thousands of whales had been slaughtered in the waters around Stellwagen Bank. Cod, too, have been fished almost to extinction. Today's population of cod is one-tenth the numbers of cod that existed just fifty years ago.

The animals around Key West also were victims of overfishing. Sailors on the *Henrietta Marie* might have taken on board green sea turtles, manatees, and Caribbean monk seals. In the early days of sail, seafarers traveling through tropical waters often captured female sea turtles as they struggled up the beaches to lay their eggs. They stored the living turtles on their backs in the holds of the ships. When fresh meat was needed on a long voyage, a turtle was brought on deck and killed.

Christopher Columbus mistook the gentle, rotund manatees for mermaids, but that didn't keep early seafarers from slaughtering these slow-moving creatures by the thousands. Today, only about three thousand manatees exist around the Florida Keys.

The Caribbean monk seal was hunted for its blubber, fur, oil, and meat ever since Western ships started exploring the region.

Columbus's crew itself killed eight "sea wolves" in 1495. Fishermen also killed monk seals, believing they were competing for their catch. The last Caribbean monk seal was seen in 1952.

Coral reefs themselves are in trouble from pollution, warming seawater temper-ature, rising sea level, and coral diseases. Even divers who come to admire the reef life in the Florida Keys and whale watchers who cheer on leaping humpback whales on Stellwagen Bank may accidentally disturb the marine life.

*   *   *

*Early sailors may have created the legend of mermaids after watching manatees nurse their babies at the surface of the sea.*

Olympic Coast

Thunder Bay

Stellwagen Bank

Cordell Bank
Gulf of the Farallones
Monterey Bay

Channel Islands

Monitor

Papahānaumokuākea ▲
Hawaiian Islands
Humpback Whale

Gray's Reef

• DESIGNATED SITES
▲ MARINE NATIONAL MONUMENT
△ PROPOSED NATIONAL MONUMENT

Fagatele Bay
(American Samoa)

Rose Atoll Marine
National Monument

Flower Garden Banks

Florida Keys
(Looe Key, Key Largo)

## ═══ Preserving Sunken Treasure: the History and the Marine Life ═══

The Florida Keys and Stellwagen Bank have become marine sanctuaries. By declaring a region of the ocean a National Marine Sanctuary, the United States government recognizes the importance of the history and marine life of an area. There are now fifteen marine protected areas where giant whales can feed, coral reefs can flourish, and lighthouses and shipwrecks can teach us about our maritime heritage. Marine sanctuaries provide safe habitats for animals that are close to extinction and protect historically significant shipwrecks. The emphasis is on research, education, and responsible use of the resources by regulating fishing, treasure hunting, and diving on coral reefs.

Although there are rules, sanctuaries are not "no trespassing" areas. Since the Florida Keys National Marine Sanctuary was established in 1990, nearly three million visitors a year dive, snorkel, boat, and fish on the largest living coral reef system in the United States. Stellwagen Bank National Marine Sanctuary was created in 1992 in order to protect the whales that come there to feed before going to the tropics to bear their young. There are rules for how close and how fast whale-watching boats may approach the whales so that the tourists can continue to view the endangered whales without harming them.

*   *   *

*National Marine Sanctuaries provide protection for the marine life and shipwrecks within their boundries.*

Each shipwreck is a mystery waiting to be solved. Even after years of study, there are many more secrets yet to be revealed. Corey Malcom of the Mel Fisher Maritime Heritage Museum says, "Exploration of the *Henrietta Marie* has gone on for thirty-five years, and we are still learning more about it." Stellwagen Bank National Marine Sanctuary's maritime archaeologists Deborah Marx and Matthew Lawrence, who explore the *Portland* every summer, agree. "Only a portion of the wreck has been recorded. Every time the Sanctuary staff returns to the site, new features are located that help us better understand the *Portland*'s historical and archaeological story."

The *Portland* is listed on the National Register of Historic Places because its archaeological remains have yielded, or will likely yield, important historical information

*The* Portland's *steam escape pipe lies on the seafloor next to the* Portland's *bow.*

about maritime New England and the techniques of shipbuilding at the time. The steamship is the best-preserved New England "overnight boat" found to date. Being in a National Marine Sanctuary prohibits "the removal, damage, disturbance, or possession of historical resources" from the *Portland* wreck site. Unlike the *Henrietta Marie*, nothing has been brought up from the wreckage of the *Portland*.

Among shipwreck explorers, a debate rages: Should artifacts be removed from a sunken ship? Items taken from the *Henrietta Marie* were made into an educational exhibit that travels to museums around the country to show what slavery was really like. Corey Malcom says it's important for others to experience what he has as the principal marine archaeologist exploring the *Henrietta Marie*. "I feel an excitement at finding an artifact for what it will teach us. And then on another level, I feel horror at what it represents, like finding a child-size shackle."

The *Henrietta Marie* now lies within the boundaries of the Florida Keys National

Marine Sanctuary. There are procedures and permits for exploring shipwrecks that weren't in place before the Sanctuary was established. Corey points out, "*Henrietta Marie* never would have been found without the exploration of treasure hunter Mel Fisher." He admits to a dilemma: Do you leave artifacts on the ocean floor or recover them and display them in a museum to tell their story? Corey responds, "There is no right answer. It's a case by case scenario. I think it's important to recover something where an artifact may be broken by waves, currents, or hurricanes, as with the *Hen-*

ABOVE: *A marine archaeologist examines timbers from the slave ship's lower hull.*

OPPOSITE: *A diver prepares to raise a cannon from the* Henrietta Marie *off the ocean floor.*

*rietta Marie*. That's a good argument for bringing it ashore." Unlike the *Portland*, which is in over three hundred feet of water, the *Henrietta Marie* lies in very shallow water. Its remains lie under only ten feet to thirty feet of water, a depth easily reached by even beginning divers. Storm waves continue to scatter artifacts from the ship far from the wreck site.

Something was added to the site of the shipwreck of the *Henrietta Marie*. A memorial facing toward Africa was placed alongside the shipwreck in 1993 by members of the National Association of Black Scuba Divers. It reads, "*Henrietta Marie*: In memory and recognition of the courage, pain, and suffering of enslaved African people. Speak her name and gently touch the souls of our ancestors."

Ships have crisscrossed the Atlantic Ocean

*Oswald Sykes of the National Association of Black Scuba Divers and journalist Michael Cottman view the monument at the site of the* Henrietta Marie.

Marine archaeologist Corey Malcom calls the *Henrietta Marie* the "anti-*Mayflower*." The trans-Atlantic crossing by the captive Africans on board the *Henrietta Marie* was in sharp contrast to the voyage undertaken by the Pilgrims, who came to the New World on the *Mayflower* in 1620 seeking religious freedom. Corey says, "People didn't come on the *Henrietta Marie* to find freedom and to express themselves. They were brought here to take away their freedom and weren't allowed to express themselves."

In 1863, President Abraham Lincoln signed the Emancipation Proclamation, which led to the abolition of slavery in the United States. Less than forty years later, many African Americans worked on ships that sailed along the coast of New England. As many as a third of the crew of the *Portland* was black. They were cooks, stewards, watchmen, and engine room operators. Through hard work and determination, they had established a thriving middle-class black community in Maine. Bob Greene of South Portland, Maine, whose great-grandmother was married to a black steward on the ship, recalled, "There was no segregation at sea. You were expected to pull your weight and it made no difference who you were."

The sinking of the *Portland* was another tragedy for the black community, one that impacted families in the region for generations. Without many of its leaders, the congregation of the black Abyssinian church in

Portland declined. As a result of the loss of their wage earners, some black families in Maine were forced to move away, and some families were split up.

Historian Walter Hickey reconstructed the passenger and crew list of the *Portland* from historical records in Boston. He found that an African-American watchman aboard the ship, John C. Whitten, left behind a wife and four children, ages six to twelve. Two years later, the 1900 U.S. population census showed his widow was residing at the "Invalids Home" in Portland, Maine, and three of the four children had been placed in foster care.

Today, the black population of Maine is on the rise, enriched by immigrants from about ten African nations. There is an effort underway to restore the historic Abyssinian church building, which closed its doors in 1917. Both black and white families are working together to preserve this symbol of hope and freedom.

*The passengers and crew who sailed on the* Portland's *last voyage represented a cross section of New England society at the end of the nineteenth century.*

for nearly five hundred years to engage in fishing, whaling, and maritime commerce. Hurricanes, snowstorms, pirates, and angry whales prevented some of them from returning home. Two thousand shipwrecks besides the *Portland* are scattered around Massachusetts Bay, and more than eight hundred shipwrecks are known to litter the reefs and sand flats off the Florida Keys.

What makes these two ships, the *Henrietta Marie* and the *Portland*, worth preserving and protecting? Each ship is an important historical monument of its era. The plants and animals that settled on each one over time represent a rich diversity of marine life from opposite ends of the ocean. Both lie within marine sanctuaries, special areas of the ocean that the United States government has determined deserve extra protection.

The story of a ship's life doesn't end with its sinking. Its decaying remains provide the beginnings of a new life. It offers opportunities for the people who will discover and study it years later and for the ocean plants and animals that will make it their home. A shipwreck proves there *can* be life after death.

RIGHT: *Marine archaeologists study artifacts scattered around a sunken ship.*

OPPOSITE: *A diver examines the plants that have transformed the silhouette of a hull of a ship at the bottom of the sea and thinks of the life that once sailed on it.*

# ❋ What Can You Do? ❋

Only a fraction of the ocean lies within the boundaries of marine sanctuaries. We don't have to depend on the federal government to protect our marine life and their sunken cities. We can each take action:

### · WRITE ·

Stellwagen Bank National Marine Sanctuary was established in part because of the letter-writing efforts of twenty thousand people, many of them schoolchildren. Write to your representatives and senators in Congress, in the state legislature, or town councilors to let them know what you think is important to protect. Letters to the editor published in your local newspaper are also a good way to spread your message.

### · CLEAN ·

Each September and October, volunteers for Coastweek Cleanups around the world pick up thousands of tons of debris. Spring is a good time to organize your own cleanup after winter storms and melting snow have deposited fishing gear and garbage on our shorelines.

### · EXPLORE ·

Some sanctuaries are hard to visit because they may be far from land. But in the Stellwagen Bank National Marine Sanctuary visitors can go on a whale watch.

In the Florida Keys National Marine Sanctuary, a Shipwreck Trail guides divers to nine sites where they can explore sunken ships. Closer to home, aquariums and nature centers exhibit similar marine life.

### · TAKE CARE OF YOUR OWN BACKYARD ·

Did you know that the single biggest source of water pollution is rainwater runoff from yards, parking lots, streets, and farms? Making sure that we all keep pesticides, fertilizers, pet wastes, cigarettes, and automobile oil out of our sewers can keep these pollutants from flowing into the ocean.

### · WHAT NOT TO DO! ·

Shipwrecks provide anchors and abodes for marine life. So why not add more? Federal, state, and city governments have dumped decommissioned ships, defective concrete pipes, millions of tires, and more than one thousand old New York City subway cars into the ocean for the stated purpose of providing recreational opportunities for divers and fishermen. Do these artificial reefs create new homes for fish, lobsters, and other bottom dwellers, or is this just a creative way of getting rid of society's junk?

# DIVING DEEPER

Bachelder, Peter Dow and Mason Philip Smith. *Four Short Blasts: The Gale of 1898 and The Loss of the Steamer* Portland. Portland, Maine: The Provincial Press, 2003.

Gibbons, Gail. *Sunken Treasure*. New York, New York: HarperCollins Children's Books, 1988.

Platt, Richard. *Eyewitness Books: Shipwrecks*. New York, New York: Alfred A. Knopf, 1997.

Sullivan, George. *Slave Ship: Story of the Henrietta Marie*. Port Salerno, Florida: Florida Classics Library, 2001.

## • VISIT ONLINE •

Stellwagen Bank National Marine Sanctuary:
  http://stellwagen.noaa.gov/

Mel Fisher Maritime Heritage Museum:
  http://www.melfisher.org/

Florida Keys Marine Sanctuary:
  http://floridakeys.noaa.gov/

*A sculpin finds a home inside the barrel of a cannon on a sunken ship.*

# GLOSSARY

**ARTIFACT** any object made by human work, such as a tool or a boat

**BIOLUMINESCENT** the ability to glow like a firefly without giving off heat the way a candle does

**CALCIUM CARBONATE** a compound found in limestone, marble, coral skeletons, crab shells, teeth, and dissolved in seawater

**CARTILAGINOUS FISH** a shark, skate, or ray. Its skeleton is made of flexible cartilage rather than hard bone

**DEBRIS FIELD** the area containing a shipwreck and artifacts from the wreck

**DRAFT** the depth of water that a ship displaces in the water

**EYESPOT** a fake eye on a fish, usually on or near the tail, to confuse predators

**GROUNDFISH**, such as cod, haddock, and flounder, that live on or near the ocean bottom

**INDIGO** a blue dye made from certain plants

**MAGNETOMETER** an instrument that can locate magnetic objects, such as anchors, cannons, and machinery, below the water's surface

**MARINE ARCHAEOLOGY** the scientific study of life and cultures of the past by examining shipwrecks and other underwater artifacts

**POLYP** the part of a coral that looks like a hollow cup with tentacles surrounding its open end

**PREDATOR** an animal that eats other animals

**SIDE-SCAN SONAR** an instrument that uses sound to produce an image of the seafloor

**TRIANGLE TRADE** the shipment of manufactured goods from Europe to Africa, where the goods were traded for human captives, who in turn were brought to the Caribbean and the Americas to be exchanged for agricultural products such as sugar, cotton, and tobacco, which were shipped back to Europe

**VICTORIAN AGE** the time when Queen Victoria ruled the British Empire, from 1837 to 1901

**ZOOXANTHELLAE** one-celled algae living in the tissues of reef-building corals

OPPOSITE: *Even if we never explore the ocean ourselves, we all have a part in protecting it.*

# ILLUSTRATION CREDITS

Mel Fisher Maritime Heritage Museum: pages 1, 2–3, 7, 8, 9, 10, 11, 12, 13, 14, 15, 16, 17, 18, 54 ,55, 56 • Jeffrey L. Rotman: pages 4, 6, 19, 20, 21, 22, 23, 24, 25, 26, 27, 43, 46, 47, 51, 58, 59, 61, 62 • Jason Henry: page 8 top • Leslie Mansmann: page 45 • Collections of the Maine Historical Society: pages 30 (#12138), 31 (*Portland Trade Journal*, Vol. 6), 57 (#13808) • Arthur Cerullo: page 32 • National Oceanic & Atmospheric Administration (NOAA)/Stellwagen Bank National Marine Sanctuary (SBNMS): pages 33, 34, 36, 51 • Richard Limeburner: page 35 • L-3 Klein Sonar Associates, Inc.: page 38 • National Oceanic & Atmospheric Administration (NOAA)/Stellwagen Bank National Marine Sanctuary (SBNMS), National Undersea Research Center—University of Connecticut (NURC-UConn), and the Science Channel: pages 39, 40, 42, 44, 53 • Maps on page 29, and on pages 41 and 52 (based on material from National Oceanic and Atmospheric Administration/National Marine Sanctuary Program) by Jason Henry • David Wiley and NOAA/ Stellwagen Bank National Marine Sanctuary: page 49.

# INDEX